# Breaking the Jar

*poems by*

# Kelsi Folsom

*Finishing Line Press*
Georgetown, Kentucky

# Breaking the Jar

Copyright © 2022 by Kelsi Folsom
ISBN 978-1-64662-946-6 First Edition
All rights reserved under International and Pan-American Copyright Conventions. No part of this book may be reproduced in any manner whatsoever without written permission from the publisher, except in the case of brief quotations embodied in critical articles and reviews.

## ACKNOWLEDGMENTS

It is with a full heart of gratitude that I acknowledge the first homes the following poems found:

*West Texas Literary Review* - "Waiting Tables"
*Red Tent Living Magazine* - "Free the Girl"
*Arise Ministries Collective* - "Breaking the Jar"
*Mothers Always Write* - "Swinging/flight"

Publisher: Leah Huete de Maines
Editor: Christen Kincaid
Cover Art: Anthony Santella
Author Photo: Wesley Folsom
Cover Design: Elizabeth Maines McCleavy

Order online: www.finishinglinepress.com
  also available on amazon.com

Author inquiries and mail orders:
Finishing Line Press
PO Box 1626
Georgetown, Kentucky 40324
USA

# Table of Contents

Prelude ............................................................................... 1
Free the Girl ....................................................................... 2
I'm a Woman Now ............................................................. 4
Youth .................................................................................. 5
Waiting Tables .................................................................... 6
Alibis ................................................................................... 7
We Like to Destroy Ourselves ........................................... 8
Addiction ............................................................................ 9
Evolution .......................................................................... 10
The Reaper ....................................................................... 11
Absolution ........................................................................ 12
Sunday School Lessons ................................................... 13
Rift .................................................................................... 14
Kyrie Eleison *(for the girls lost in the streets of Kitwe, Zambia)* .... 15
Possession ........................................................................ 17
Flashback ......................................................................... 18
The Escape Room ............................................................ 19
Baggage ............................................................................ 21
Blood Daughter ............................................................... 22
Breaking the Jar ............................................................... 23
Sutured ............................................................................. 24
The Very Good Body ....................................................... 25
Swinging (flight) .............................................................. 26
Postlude ........................................................................... 28

*For every girl whose voice was silenced
and every girl whose body was shamed.*

*For every girl whose dreams went quiet
and every girl whose fire was tamed.*

*For every girl who lost her innocence
and every girl who thought she was to blame.*

*For every woman who's never forgotten
and every woman reclaiming her name.*

**Prelude**
> *from "The Wounds of Jesus" by Rev. C.C. Lovelace*
> *as recorded by Zora Neale Hurston*

One angel took the flinches of God's eternal power
And bled the veins of the earth
One angel that stood at the gate with a flaming sword
Was so well pleased with his power
Until he pierced the moon with his sword
And she ran down in blood

**Free the Girl**

I usually want to look away,
but this time,
I couldn't.

The lights were on
and my alibis were
nowhere to be found.

Just me with a flashlight
not making a sound
and her, just a whimper of a girl.

She didn't have a choice,
but now she does.

"NO!"

She bellows to the script of the night
"Take it back, I've a new story now."

But first turn the page
and hold what was there.

Rage: the thorn in her flesh.

The indescribable flip of a switch
inside a wild body,
a dropped expression
feral in its pain.

Like a runaway train this need for destruction
is fueled and refueled, a reordering
of reality to mirror her spirit-
the girl whose power was removed.

Too soon the moon showed her face
and took up residence where once there was only space.

The independent girl
sank to the bottom line

shut her mouth,
clasped her hands
closed off to the light.

The four walls should have been her bedchamber,
but they changed into iron rods of self-doubt and pity.

"Learn to love it," *they* said.

"Try and make it pretty" *she* thought
as her small palm sought heat from the stone.

Eventually the darkness closes her eyes
and she forgets what it means to want out.

A window opens every once in a while
and she screams like the air might turn into a rope
she can cling to and leave,

find a hope with no catch,
no caveat to take away her name.

Perhaps now she knows why she wants to escape:
to be the only one who actually has a say.

**I'm A Woman Now**

My breath caught
when I saw the stain,
pure white Hanes telling
me I'm dangerous now.

A baby could grow
in the deepest dark of me
so lo and behold
the unfolding spring.

The boys would know,
they can smell fertility
snicker smart at the soft geography
tethering each wing.

I'm a woman now
but what I didn't know,
is that made me unstoppable.

Watch me.

**Youth**

Her legs were crossed
like a pair of shears

waiting for the soft touch
of spring to unfold them.

Lips flush with questions
she never knew to ask.

Eyes quick to rest
near the exits.

**Waiting Tables**

I watch
as beans from Ka'anapali
crumble into coarse sand.
4 Tablespoons are leveled off,
saturated with water
just shy of boiling.

Honeywheat bloom sends me smiling towards my guests.

"Give it about 4 minutes
then press the plunger.
Enjoy your coffee."
I walk away proud
of my confidence,
proud of my skill
to present and instruct.

I straighten my name
printed on plastic
and re-tuck the denim
slipping out
of black cotton.

"Order up!"
pulls my ear to the kitchen,
but I pause
as his stare finds a way
to un-tuck
what I've just done.

I fetch the slimy scramble
and the sweet, steaming pancakes,
Careful not to burn my fingertips
or linger at the counter.

## Alibis

I fear pleasure,
the unplugged "yes!"
of hunger,
the well-dressed cousin
of pain.

*I won't be fooled.*

They are the same name.

## We Like to Destroy Ourselves

I slid into the
        sandals by the door
kicked off in pursuit
        of liquor and solitaire.

In spades, loneliness
        finds its hunger
nestled atop a
        parcel of ribs.

It's done,
        but it never is,
this berating and
        leaning towards

that which we say we don't know,

        *(but we do)*

It never is.

## Addiction

I am afraid of hunger,
the bottomless way it lingers
even after satiation it lurks
near the doorway,
assessing every weakness.

*What if I am never filled?*
*What if I am never complete?*

### Evolution (fight or flight)

You'd think by the eighth attempt at a heart,
I'd have arrived at the perfect machination.

I should have smoothed out the weird muscle by now,
but a wayward memory constricts in the worst way.

Too large and I burn, my face flushing red,
the wheelhouse of memory too raucous to bear.

Too small and I freeze, no kindling for the hearth,
peering slit-eyed through the frosty windowpanes.

I'm sorry, but tell me—which is worse?
Burning or freezing: they're both preludes to death.

## The Reaper

Death doesn't care
how good you are.
She knocks
ever so softly,
like maybe this time
you will open the door
and pour her a cup of tea.

She just wants to
get to know you,
sit at your table
and comment on
the beauty of the
floral placemats you
found for a dollar
at a garage sale
down the street.

She's so nice
and wise,
seems to know a little
something about
everything and every one.

She peers at you through
the steam curling around
her eyelashes from the
porcelain cup you steeped
a bag of Earl Grey in.

Before you know it,
she clasps your hand
and gives it
a good squeeze.

She's never going to leave.

**Absolution**

What if I sat here drinking,
numbing the distance
between myself?

What if I sat here fuming,
throwing curses around
like seed?

What if I beat me senseless,
forcing all the "rules"
I'm "supposed" to?

Would anything change?
Would my heart concede?
I have trouble remembering my name.

**Sunday School Lessons**

It's the cool of the porcelain
I cannot forget,
the rigid prints of "pervert"
on my thighs.

It's the mouth agape
I can't seem to shut,
no sound
able to escape.

It's the eyes of sincerity
asking me what's wrong
when my lips quiver
at the slightest sight of you.

It's the lessons you taught me
behind the flannel graphs
that linger
long after the telling.

**Rift**

The earth has a grief to release,
an ancient sorrow to tear
through the geological layers

Plant a foot in her heart
let her blood give you wisdom

Like misty whispers dripping
from the blades of her hair

She's been waiting out humanity
since the beginning of time,

Absorbing the storms
of each heart full of lies—

"We're listening, mother earth,
tell us why you cry?"

## Kyrie Eleison
### *(for the girls lost in the streets of Kitwe, Zambia)*

Sweat wept from every pore,
branding patterns of salt
across the bridge of her nose,
cheeks bright lips
upturned in defiance,
even defeat wouldn't
dare keep her down.

*Kyrie eleison*

The back of a blade
Cleaved breast from
Breastbone mixing
Work and play in a torrid
Blend of lust and supremacy,
boy>girl
every time the
Geography of a soul in
the judgment seat of gender.

*Kyrie eleison*

A shadow says so much
of what was there
of what should be
of what could be
of what would be…
Like the shroud of Turin
She has made her mark
With the word of her sweat
the weight of her flesh.

*Kyrie eleison*

The wind will remember
the dreams in her heart
to heal broken bodies
with skill and determination,
a sweet dream tucked
in the corner of her will
never to see the light of day.

*Kyrie eleison*

These words will bring
her battered soul
to the heavenlies
to sing back with
the blood of the knowing moon
every sorrow mother earth
took on deep within her womb.

*Kyrie eleison*

**Possession**

It's interesting the ways
a woman's body can sin
without her even knowing.

Her softness fells
the iron wills of
men to prevent
their eyes from
lusting but isn't
this the mountain
of God? Shouldn't
the crown of God's
creation (his words,
not mine) be a
harbinger of pride,
a vessel of glory?

She is good
she was made good
so the problem is
not the body
but the sight—
that's where the
real blight is—

Awe is blinded
into a hunger
for possession,
something Jesus
tells over and over
we are to let go of.

**Flashback**

Rage appears like a hidden hunter:
calculated and assured.

Stagnant water gushes from
his throat, tight and stunted

like the opening of a geyser
chokes the blood of mother earth.

What is it? Can we yank it out?
A rock of resistance or
a prayer in the drought?

Maybe it's a notebook full of names
calling every man a crook.

So a rip of justification
makes a fault jutting through

the prairie lands, like a
sword that's left it's handle.

## The Escape Room

The sound wave of the monster
is explosive rage—
Betrayal is his name,
violation his bent.

He cannot rest,
cannot sleep,
the bread crumb of justice
just out of reach.

What does it look like?
A murder, I think,
but of who or of what?
The name escapes me.

It's the love child of fear,
disgust, and powerless;
the feel of a dusty boot
brandishing your neck.

You're pinned
but you know
you are smart
or at least fast,
but alas,
the exhaustion
starts to win.

"How dare you smear
your sickness over me?
You're a coward,
and your fistfuls
of innocence tell me,

I'm a wonder
you could never stomach down

so

take it all back,
I don't answer to you!"
and I leave
on the coattails
of some courage.

My footsteps echo loud,
shatter passageways of time
building up to freedom,

now

I'm fully mine.

## Baggage

Show me how to nurture
and be nurtured, how
to rise up into my skin
and feel it all in real time.

Tell me how to know
the path is sure
and I am free,
how to drop the
records of old melodies
tripping up my feet.

Help me rename
bone by bone
every word I thought
I stood for,

Help me tear down
stone by stone
every lie I thought
I lived for.

## Blood Daughter

I pierce my heart
on the crux of Jesus,
falling on his goodness
with the frailty
of my weakness.

Calling out his name
in desperate piety while
profane remembrances,
curses for this broken world
billow from my bones.

It's impossible,
this human bent
wrapped around each
axle of a noble dream
esteemed for just a moment
clinking flutes of champagne
held by who we hope to be.

**Breaking the Jar**
*Luke 7:38*

I sit at your feet and weep,
                      weep,
Weep into your heavenly hems.

Soaking through barriers
shameless, again
My sorrow has no feet.

I rend my heart before you
seeking all you are
to be all I am not
And cannot…

I lay in your wounds
safe and sound
Profound,
your love is beautiful wine,

So fine,
and I
Am lost again
in same-ness.

**Sutured**

How could perfection
step foot in this mire,
grab a seat and a scone
and call it good?

How could a visit
in grave clothes become
sequined Bodycons
and spinning disco balls?

How could a broken
body open a wound
and find foaming wine
in the depths

making peace,
stitch by stitch,
with the shadows
writing letters

on my flesh?

## The Very Good Body

It's like a temple I walk around in
breathing mists like salvation's tonic.

There's a line, a streak of pain
that surrounds the sleeping dreams,

an electric fence of fierce resistance
keeping all the beasts at bay.

This home is too precious
borne out of fire.

It's steel has been tested
no weapon can divide it.

What has died and found new life
can't be stopped by stilted pride.

Heartbeats *thump thump* from the stone
even a rock is too soft for this love.

Human hands cannot lay hold
the hope that finds asylum here.

**Swinging (flight)**

The grey chain
wrapped
in blue ribbon
holds me close,
pacing my flight
like a pendulum.

Hair brushed by
salty wind
blowing through
the oak trees,
laughing lines
grooved along
the branches.

To my right
the next generation
subdues the earth,
curls bright
with possibilities-

At her feet,
endless territory
to walk and call
her own.

At her back,
sinewy love
swallowing up a
crinkled face with joy.

In her chest,
a window frosted
with snowy drops
of new life.

Inside,
a heavy heart
grows a little lighter,
as a little girl leans back
to catch the sunlight.

**Postlude**

*And de sun*
*Batted her fiery eyes and put on her judgment robe*
*And laid down in de cradle of eternity*
*And rocked herself into sleep and slumber*

*-from "The Wounds of Jesus" by Rev. C.C. Lovelace*
*as recorded by Zora Neale Hurston*

**K**elsi Folsom is a singer, seminary student, wife, and mom to four kids making her home in Lima, Ohio. Her poems and essays are published in *The Caribbean Writer, Snapdragon Journal, Wildroof Journal, Coffee and Crumbs, Voices de la luna, Grit and Virtue, Mothers Always Write,* and elsewhere. She is the author of *Buried in the Margins* (Finishing Line Press, 2020) and the poetry chapbook *Words the Dirt Meant to Share* (Desert Willow Press, 2018). She is currently pursuing an M.A. in Theopoetics and Writing from Bethany Theological Seminary, and relishes conversations about art, culture, and faith. She believes God's love changes everything, and thrives on encouraging others to live embodied lives of purpose and peace. When she isn't cooking for family and friends, she enjoys thrifting, doing puzzles, getting lost in a good novel, and occasionally putting her B.M. in Voice Performance to good use. Hang out with her on Instagram @kelsifolsom and at her website www.kelsifolsom.com where you can sign up for her bi-monthly newsletter, *The Shameless Beauty Digest*

www.ingramcontent.com/pod-product-compliance
Lightning Source LLC
LaVergne TN
LVHW041510070426
835507LV00012B/1476